Peyo

SMURF Adventures

Romeo and Smurfette

and 12 OTHER SMURFY STORIES

Written by DELPORTE and PEYO

Translated by Anthea Bell and Derek Hockridge

Random House New York

Romeo and Smurfette

Once upon a time, a hundred Smurfs were
living peacefully and happily together.
Until along came a Smurfette...
But that was another story.

You were asking what became of her?
She's fine.
Every now and then she comes back to
visit the village, and the stories you are
about to read will show you she
hasn't changed.

Peyo & Y. Delporte

Romeo and Smurfette

49

Smurf, smurf, nothing but smurf the whole time.
And then as likely as not you have to smurf it all over again.

However...

Many hands make light smurf.
And all smurf and no play makes Smurf a dull smurf.
So how about a bit of...

Smurfery

LOOK, PAPA SMURF! A THIEF SMURFED ONE OF MY CAKES THIS MORNING! THAT REALLY SMURFS THE BISCUIT!

I'LL UNSMURF THE CULPRIT. ELEMENTARY, MY DEAR SMURFSON!

THANKS, PAPA SMURF.

YOU TWO, WHAT WERE YOU SMURFING THIS MORNING?

I WAS PLAYING SMURFBALL WITH HIM!

HE WAS PLAYING SMURFBALL WITH ME!

I WAS SMURFING GROUCHY SMURF SOME GOOD ADVICE, PAPA SMURF, BECAUSE YOU SHOULD ALWAYS LISTEN TO YOUR ELDERS AND BETTERS AND...

I NEVER BET!

OI WERE SMURFING IN THEY FIELDS, OI WERE, LISTENING TO POET SMURF!

I WAS HERE WITH FARMER SMURF, SMURFING MY POETIC MUSE!

ME TOO!

I SMURFED IN LATE TODAY!

I WAS PRACTICING MY TRUMPET.

I WAS STOPPING UP MY EARS!

I WAS CATCHING A COLD!

I WAS SMURFING A DEAR LITTLE CROCHET CAP!

HMM... BY A PROCESS OF ELIMINSMURFATION...

WELL, PAPA SMURF, DID YOU UNSMURF THE THIEF?

YES.

ONLY ONE SMURF HAS NO ALIBI! SO IT MUST HAVE BEEN HIM!

WHO?

...ME!

!

PFFF!...

I'M SMURFED TO THE BACK TEETH... REALLY BORED TO SMURF!

YAAAWN...

?

HULLO?

GO ON, SMURF OFF, YOU LUCKY SMURF, YOU!

REALLY? AT LAST!!

WE OUGHT REALLY TO ASK SCULPTOR SMURF TO SMURF US SOME LITTLE FIGURES FOR OUR GAMES OF CHESS...

CHEAT? ARE YOU NUTS?

YES, CHESS-NUTS...

OH.

...SO I TOLD HIM THAT WAS NO REASON TO GET ON HIS SMURF HORSE WHEN HE SPOKE TO ME...

SMURF TO KING SIX...

CHECK!

I'VE BEEN TAKEN! I'VE BEEN TAKEN! TRA LA LA!

LOOK HERE, A SMURF'S SMURF IS HIS CASTLE!

57

DEAR ME, DEAR ME, WHAT LANGUAGE!

IT'S THAT SMURFING MALLET. I SMURFED MY FOOT WITH IT, PAPA SMURF!

THAT'S NO REASON TO SMURF SUCH NAUGHTY WORDS! GO AND SMURF OUT YOUR MOUTH WITH SOAP! GET A SMURF ON!

FRRRRR FRRRR FRRR

VERY WELL, AND DON'T LET ME SMURF YOU SAYING NAUGHTY WORDS AGAIN, UNDERSMURF?

UNDERSMURF PAPA SMURF!

... BECAUSE PAPA SMURF SAYS WE SHOULD NEVER PUT THE SMURF BEFORE THE SMURF, AND PAPA SMURF KNOWS WHAT HE'S SMURFING ABOUT, AND IT WAS PAPA SMUR...

...UUUURF!

PAF!

OH, BLOW! I'VE HAD ENOUGH OF THIS!

MORE THAN ENOUGH! I'M GOING ON STRIKE!

I ASK YOU! I CAN NEVER GET A SMURF IN SMURFWAYS WITHOUT SOME SMURF COMING AND SMURFING ME OVER THE SMURF!

BUT I'M GOING TO TELL PAPA SMURF, AND THEY'LL ALL BE SMURFY, BECAUSE THEY WON'T GET ANY SMURF CREAM FOR PUDDING AND IT JUST SMURFS THEM RIGHT, BECAUSE IT'S BETTER TO BE SMURF THAN SORRY AND WHEN I SMUR...

...UUUURF!

PAF

86

LIFE HERE IS CALM AND PEACEFUL. WE ARE, OF COURSE, IN THE SMURF VILLAGE.

YUM, YUM! WHO WANTS A SMURF OF MY CAKE?

IT'S... !?

WHAT SMURF WENT AND SMURFED ON MY CAKE?

THAT BIRD! IT'S GOT A LETTER IN ITS, SMURF!

LOOK WHAT YOU'VE SMURFED! AREN'T YOU ASHAMED OF YOUR-SMURF?

IT'S FROM THE SMURFETTE! QUICK — WE MUST GO AND TELL PAPA SMURF!

PAPA SMURF! PAPA SMURF! A LETTER FROM THE SMURFETTE!

I HATE LETTERS!

Dear little Smurfs, I have something very, very important to smurf you. I'm coming to see you tomorrow. Smurfette.

IT'S FROM HER!

SHE'S COMING TO SEE US!

QUICK! MY MOST SMURFISTICATED SCENT!

PSSSST PSSSST

I'LL SMURF HER A LOVELY PRESENT!

SHE LIKES SMURF TART WITH LOTS OF SMURFED CREAM!

I DON'T UNDERSTAND! MY ARROW NEVER USUALLY MISSES ITS SMURF!

IT DIDN'T THIS TIME EITHER, SMURF YOU!

LET'S RESMURF TO ZERO. TO SMURF OUT OF THE SMURF'S GRAVITY, THE BEST EQUATION IS $T = -2(R+H)$, WHICH MEANS I CAN...

WHAT A LOVELY MOON, I'VE SMURFED OUT! I'LL CUT ALL THE OTHERS OUT WITH THIS!

AND NEXT DAY...

LOOK, SMURFETTE, HERE'S THE MOON! NOW WE CAN GET SMURFED!

DON'T BELIEVE A SMURF HE SAYS! HERE'S THE REAL MOON!

ER... I DIDN'T QUITE SMURF IT, BUT WILL THIS DO?

NO, NO! YOU'RE ALL DEAR LITTLE SMURFS, BUT YOU'VE NONE OF YOU SMURFED ME WHAT I WANTED. I'M CRYING FOR THE MOON!

ANYWAY, I THINK PERHAPS I'M RATHER YOUNG TO GET SMURFED AFTER ALL! I'LL THINK IT OVER!

I'LL BE BACK LATER! GOODBYE FOR NOW!

SHE... SHE'S GONE.

SNIFF!

COME ALONG, SMURFS, DON'T BE DOWNSMURFED! SHE SAID SHE'D BE BACK. SO LET'S MAKE SMURF WHILE THE SUN SHINES... NOT TO MENTION THE MOON.

YOU KNOW, PAPA SMURF MAY HAVE A POINT!

YOU'RE RIGHT. WE LOVE HER EVEN MORE WHEN SHE ISN'T AROUND!

COME ON, LET'S SMURF A PARTY!

YIPPEE! THAT'S A SMURF IDEA!

PHEW! IT ALL SMURFED OUT FOR THE BEST!

I'VE GOT THIS SMURFLY CAKE! WHO WANTS A SMURF OF MY CAKE?

I HATE CAKES WHEN THEY'VE ALREADY GOT THE BIRD!

THE END

4

Traveling Smurf

THE LITTLE SMURFS LEAD A HAPPY, PEACEFUL LIFE IN THEIR VILLAGE...

THEY ARE ALL CHEERFUL AND GOOD-NATURED AS THEY GO ABOUT THEIR BUSINESS...

EXCEPT FOR ONE. HE IS SAD AND MELANCHOLY, A DREAMER... HE IS NOT AT ALL LIKE THE OTHER SMURFS.

HI, SMURF! COMING TO PLAY SMURFBALL WITH US?

NO, I DON'T WANT TO.

FUNNY SORT OF SMURF... NEVER WANTS TO PLAY SMURF WITH ANYONE!

NEXT MORNING...

GOODBYE, EVERYSMURF!

COME SMURF SOON!

SURE I WILL!

HERE, TAKE THIS MAGIC WHISTLE! IF EVER YOU FIND YOURSELF IN DANGER, JUST SMURF IT, AND YOU'LL BE BACK HERE RIGHT AWAY!

OH, THANKS, PAPA SMURF!

YIPPEE! HERE GOES!

THE WIDE WORLD LIES BEFORE ME! I SHALL SMURF HIGH MOUNTAIN RANGES, CROSS SEAS AND DESERTS. I'M OFF ON A ROUND SMURF OF THE WORLD!

5

AFTER WALKING ALL DAY...

EVENING... I MUST SMURF FOR SOMEWHERE TO SPEND THE NIGHT!

THIS LOOKS LIKE A GOOD PLACE!

I GUESS I SHALL SMURF LIKE A LOG AMONG THESE TREES!

CRACK

WHAT WAS THAT?

TOO-WHIT TOO-WOO

WH...WHAT ARE ALL THESE NOISES? OOOH... I DON'T LIKE IT!

I... I COULD ALWAYS SMURF THE WHISTLE... NO, I WON'T! THE OTHERS WOULD ALL SMURF AT ME!

I WAS SO COMFY IN MY OWN BED IN THE VILLAGE! OH, WHY DID I LEAVE? SNIFF... IT'S NOT SUCH SMURF OUT IN THE WIDE WORLD AFTER ALL!

FINALLY, JUST BEFORE DAWN, THE EXHAUSTED LITTLE SMURF GETS TO SLEEP...

6

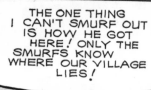

12

BY SMURF, THIS IS CATASMURFIC! THAT CAT WILL EAT HIM ALIVE!

QUICK, LET'S SMURF! WE MAY BE IN TIME YET!

WAIT FOR ME! I'LL COME WITH YOU!

MEANWHILE...

IF ONLY I COULD SMURF MYSELF FREE BEFORE GARGAMEL GETS BACK! THEN WE'D SEE WHICH WAY THE CAT SMURFS!

HMMMPH...

MIAOOOW!

AZRAEL!!

HELP! HE'S GOING TO SMURF ME ALIVE!

FASTER! FASTER!

13

14

AND THAT EVENING, TRAVELING SMURF IS DANCING WITH THE REST OF THEM... HE HAS BECOME A SMURF JUST LIKE THE OTHER SMURFS.

17

The END